Duos für klassische Gitarre 1

Duets for Classical Guitar 1

14 Stücke bearbeitet von
Pieces arranged by
Fabian Payr

Sy. 2405

RICORDI

Duos für klassische Gitarre 1
Duets for Classical Guitar 1

14 Stücke bearbeitet von | 14 pieces arranged by
Fabian Payr

Sy. 2405

Impressum

© 2020 by G. RICORDI & CO. Bühnen- und Musikverlag GmbH, Berlin (für alle Länder | for all countries)

Notensatz | Engraving: Fabian Payr, Burkhard Osteneck

Umschlagfoto | Front Cover Image: iStock by Getty Images

ISMN 979-0-2042-2405-0

Vorwort

Bearbeitungen klassischer Werke für Gitarre solo sind bereits in großer Zahl erhältlich; sie sind aber oft so anspruchsvoll zu spielen, dass sie die Fähigkeiten der meisten Gitarristen übersteigen. Vorliegende *Duos für klassische Gitarre* umgehen dieses Problem: Der originale Notentext für unterschiedlichste Besetzungen – von Klavier solo über verschiedene Kammermusikformationen bis hin zu Chor und Orchester – wird hier zwei Gitarren anvertraut, was im Vergleich zu einer Solobearbeitung zwei jeweils deutlich angenehmer spielbare Parts ermöglicht. Auf diese Weise werden berühmte Kompositionen aus diversen Stilepochen Gitarristen teils erstmals zugänglich gemacht.

Die Sammlung in zwei Bänden (Band 1: eher leicht, Band 2: etwas schwieriger) umfasst Werke von Bach, Mozart, Schumann, Elgar und vielen anderen – genau das Richtige für alle, die einmal über den Tellerrand des gewohnten Gitarrenrepertoires schauen möchten. Enthalten sind aber auch bekannte Stücke aus der anspruchsvollen Sololiteratur für Gitarre, etwa von Tárrega oder Sor, die dank der Aufteilung des Notentextes auf zwei Spieler schon von weniger fortgeschrittenen Gitarristen erarbeitet werden können.

Ich hoffe, hiermit einen wesentlichen Beitrag zur Repertoireerweiterung klassischer Gitarristen zu leisten und zugleich zu kammermusikalischen Erfahrungen im Duospiel zu motivieren.

Fabian Payr

Preface

Although numerous arrangements of classical pieces for solo guitar are already available, they are often so challenging to play that they are beyond the capabilities of most guitarists. The classical guitar duets presented here completely do away with this problem: the instrumentation of the original score—from solo piano to different chamber, choral and orchestral ensembles—is shared between two guitars, which makes for significantly more 'playable' parts in comparison to a solo arrangement. Famous compositions from various eras and in a variety of styles are accessible to guitarists, in some cases for the first time.

The collection, in two volumes (vol. 1: quite easy, vol. 2: somewhat more difficult) includes works by Bach, Mozart, Schumann, Elgar and many others. It is perfect for anyone who wants to look further than the standard guitar repertoire. It also includes well-known pieces from the demanding solo guitar repertoire—for example by Tárrega and Sor—which can be played by less advanced guitarists thanks to the 'division of labour' between two instruments.

It is my hope in producing this collection that it makes a significant contribution to the expansion of the repertoire for classical guitarists and, at the same time, that it motivates them to gain chamber music experience in duo playing.

Fabian Payr

Inhalt | Content

Lascia ch'io pianga

Arie aus der Oper | Aria from the opera *Rinaldo*

Georg Friedrich Händel (1685–1759)

Arr.: Fabian Payr

Edition Ricordi

Mouvement de prière religieuse

op. 31,23

Fernando Sor (1778–1839)

Arr.: Fabian Payr

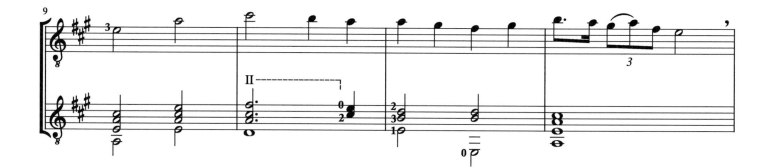

Edition Ricordi

Sy. 2405

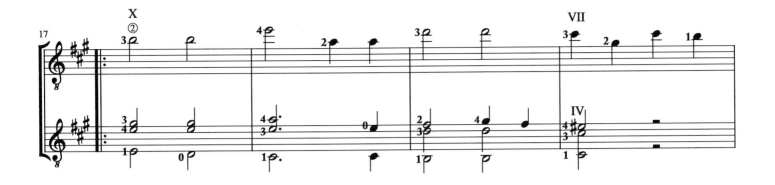

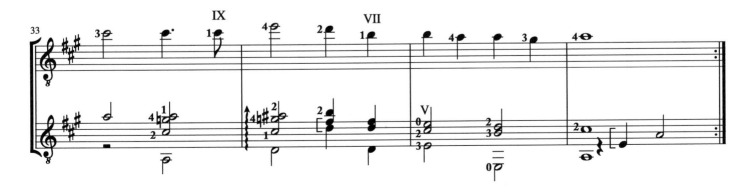

Moderato

op. 35,17

Fernando Sor (1778–1839)
Arr.: Fabian Payr

Edition Ricordi

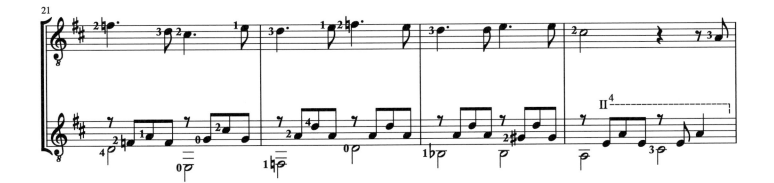

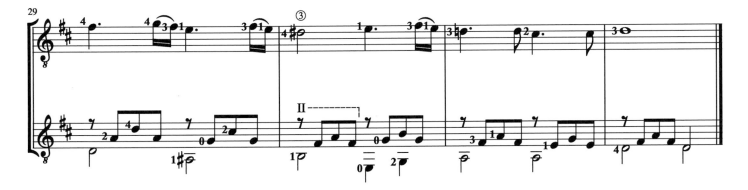

Allegretto

nach | after Fernando Sor (op. 35,22)

Fabian Payr (*1963)

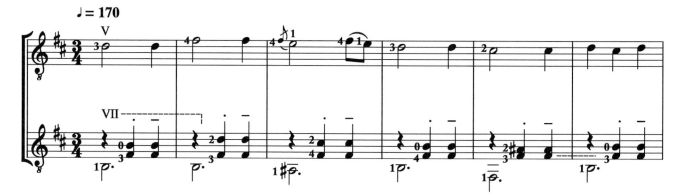

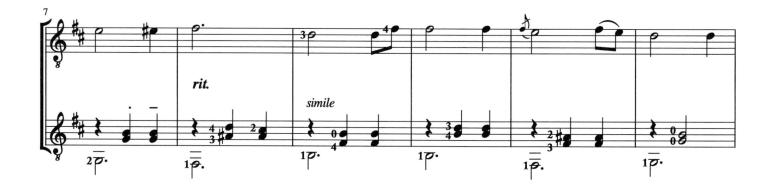

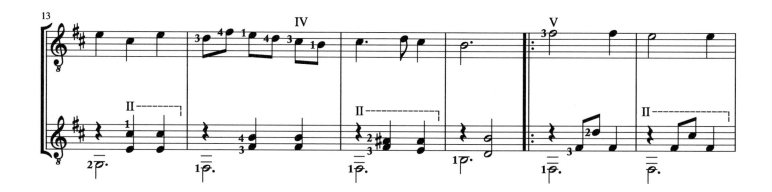

Edition Ricordi

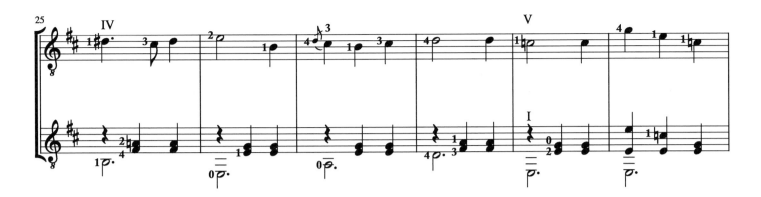

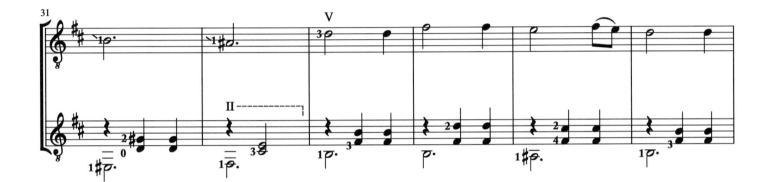

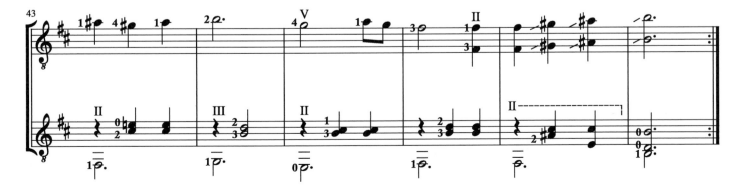

Von fremden Ländern und Menschen

aus | from *Kinderszenen* op. 15,1

Robert Schumann (1810–1856)

Arr.: Fabian Payr

Edition Ricordi

Sy. 2405

Lágrima

Preludio

Francisco Tárrega (1852–1909)
Arr.: Fabian Payr

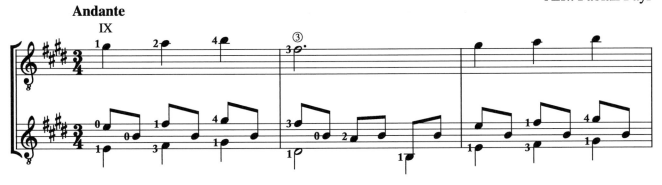

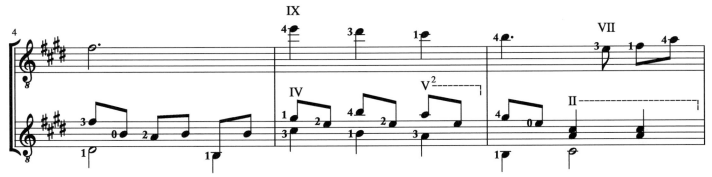

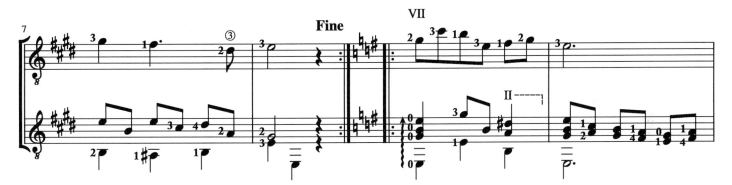

To a Wild Rose

Edward MacDowell (1860–1908)
Arr.: Fabian Payr

With simple tenderness

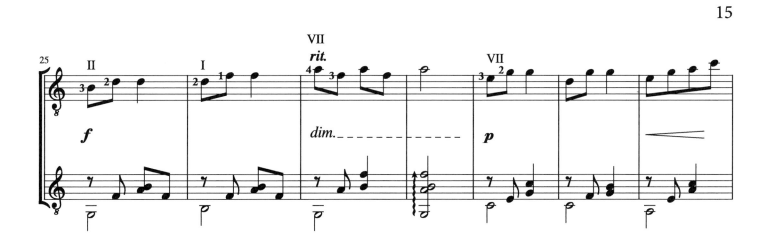

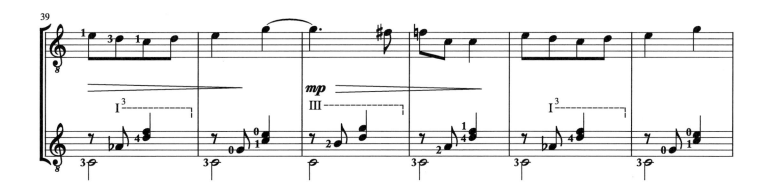

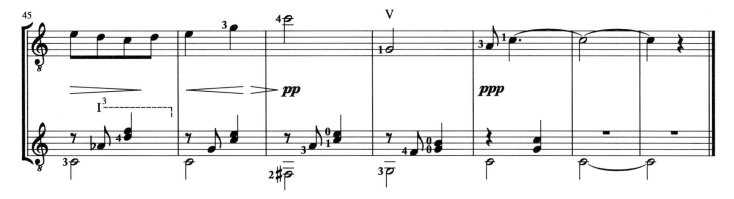

Sung Outside the Prince's Door

aus | from *Forgotten Fairytales* op. 4,1

Edward MacDowell (1860–1908)

Arr.: Fabian Payr

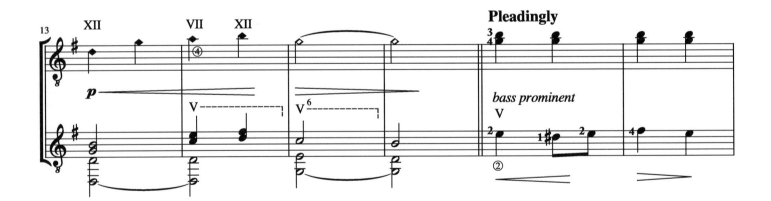

Edition Ricordi

Sy. 2405

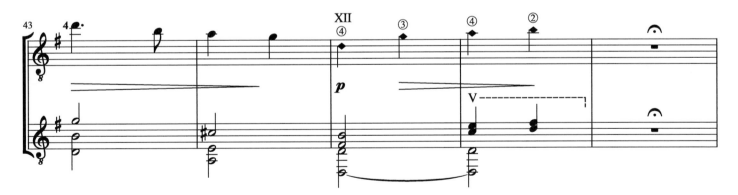

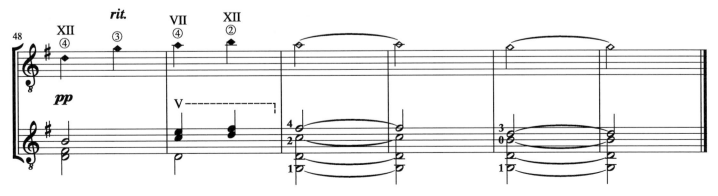

Falling Leaves

Ballade | Ballad

Peter Reimer (* 1964)
Arr.: Fabian Payr

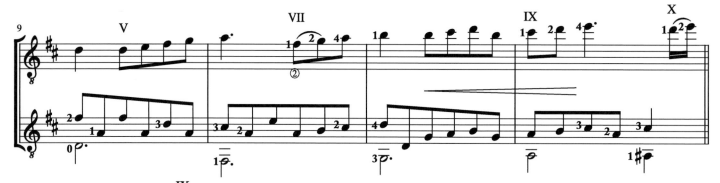

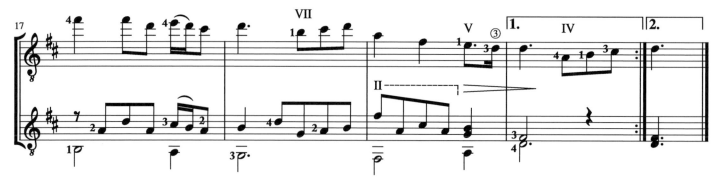

Edition Ricordi   Sy. 2405

Aus: Album *What's Left* von Peter Reimer
© 2017 by Verlag Peter Reimer

Berceuse aux étoiles

aus | from *Petite Suite en quinze images*

Jacques Ibert (1890–1962)

Arr.: Fabian Payr

Aus: Jacques Ibert: „Petite Suite" en quinze images

L'Adieu

Jacques Ibert (1890–1962)
Arr.: Fabian Payr

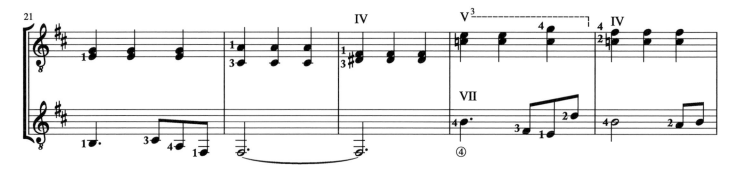

Aus: Jacques Ibert: „Petite Suite" en quinze images

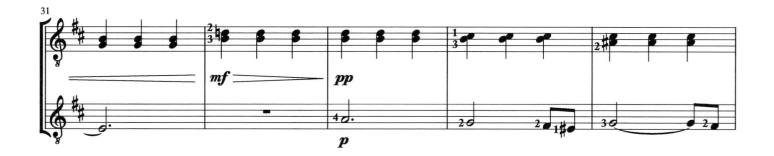

* = Überstreckung | stretch

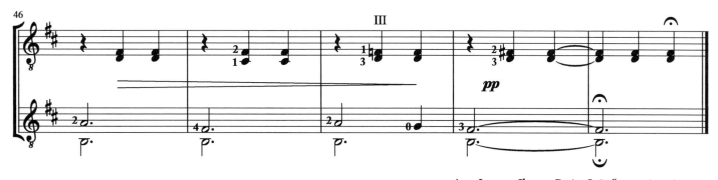

Aus: Jacques Ibert: „Petite Suite" en quinze images

Ave verum corpus

KV 618

Wolfgang Amadeus Mozart (1756–1791)

Arr.: Fabian Payr

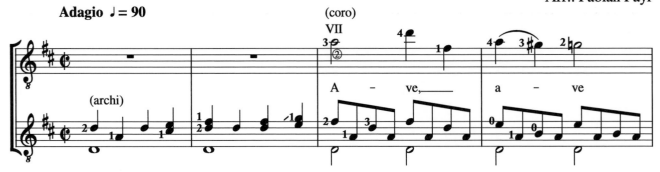

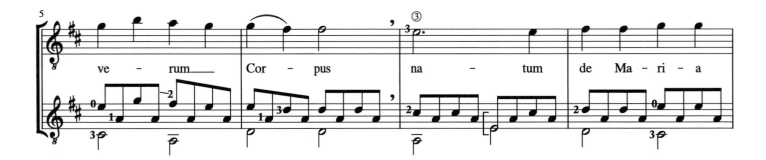

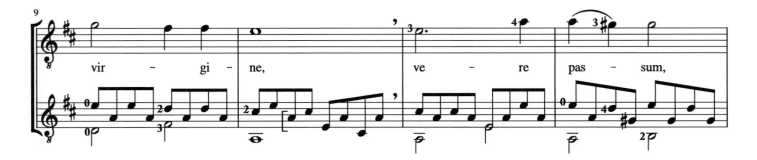

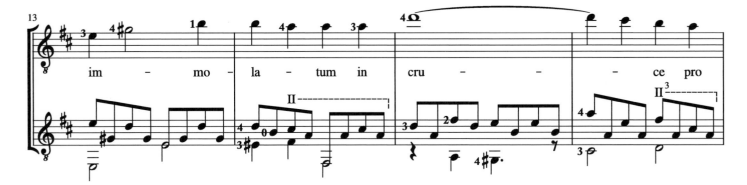

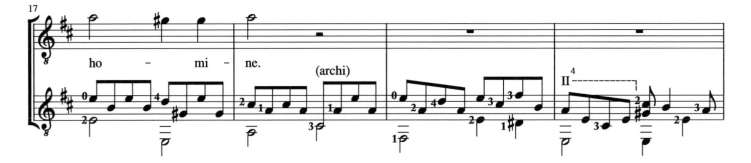

Edition Ricordi

Sy. 2405

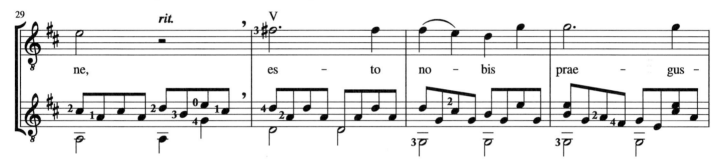

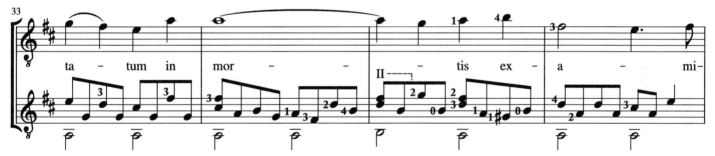

Prelude to Olga

Jorge Morel (* 1931)
Arr.: Fabian Payr

Edition Ricordi Sy. 2405

Farewell

Fabian Payr (*1962)

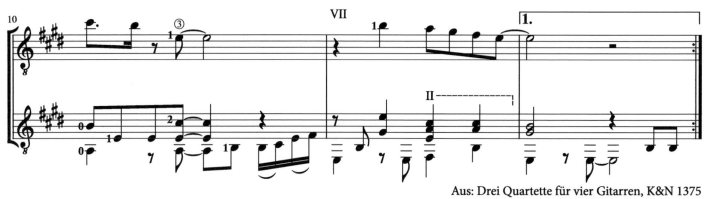

Aus: Drei Quartette für vier Gitarren, K&N 1375

Edition Ricordi

Sy. 2405

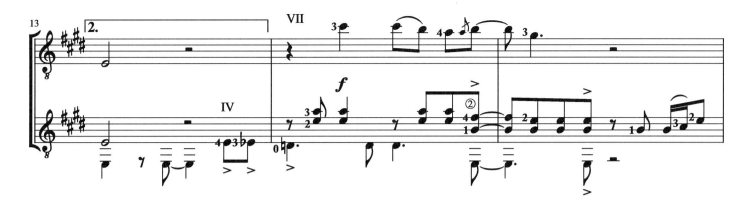

D.S. con rip. al Fine

Edition Ricordi

Sy. 2405

Aus: Drei Quartette für vier Gitarren, K&N 1375
© 2003 by Verlag Hubertus Nogatz (www.nogatz.de)

RICORDI

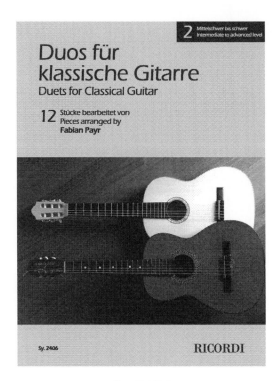

Sy. 2406

Siciliano (J. S. Bach)

Complaint (F. Payr)

Fanfarinette (J.-P. Rameau)

Les Sauvages (J.-P. Rameau)

La livri (J.-P. Rameau)

Le Tambourin (J.-P. Rameau)

Gavotta (A. Ariosti)

Klaviersonate Nr. 17 | Piano Sonata No. 17 (W. A. Mozart)

Lied ohne Worte op. 67,6 (F. Mendelssohn Bartholdy)

Salut d'amour (E. Elgar)

Les tendres plaintes (J.-P. Rameau)

Gran Vals (F. Tárrega)